ALZHEIMER'S DISEASE

How to care for your loved ones
affected with Alzheimer's

Lisa W. Cyrus

ALZHEIMER'S DISEASE

Table of contents

Chapter 1: Understanding Alzheimer's illness
  What Causes Alzheimer's Disease?
  Alzheimer's as a Continuum
  Symptoms of Alzheimer's
  Alzheimer's and the brain
  Research and progress

Chapter 2: Stages of Alzheimer's illness
  Preclinical Alzheimer's disease
  Mild cognitive impairment (MCI) owing to Alzheimer's disease
  Mild dementia linked to Alzheimer's disease
  Moderate dementia related to Alzheimer's disease
  Severe dementia related to Alzheimer's disease
  Rate of progression through Alzheimer's disease stages

Chapter 3: CAREGIVING

Chapter 4: Food and Eating

Chapter 1: Understanding Alzheimer's illness

Alzheimer's disease is an irreversible, degenerative brain condition that steadily damages memory and cognitive abilities and, finally, the ability to carry out the simplest activities. It is the most prevalent cause of dementia in older persons. While dementia is increasingly frequent as individuals get older, Alzheimer's is not a natural aspect of aging.

Alzheimer's is a disease that robs individuals of their memories. At first, individuals have a hard time recalling recent occurrences, yet they could readily recall things that occurred years before.

As time goes on, new symptoms might arise, including:

Trouble focusing

A hard difficulty accomplishing regular things
Feeling puzzled or dissatisfied, particularly at night
Dramatic mood swings — outbursts of rage, anxiety, and melancholy
Feeling confused and getting lost easy
Physical difficulties, such as an awkward walk or poor coordination

Trouble communicating
People with Alzheimer's could forget their loved ones. They could forget how to dress, eat themselves, and use the bathroom.

The condition causes brain tissue to break away over time. It mainly occurs in adults over age 65.

A person may live with Alzheimer's disease for only a few years or a few decades. More typically, though, individuals live with it for roughly 9 years. About 1 in 8 adults age 65 and above has the condition. Women are more likely to have it than males.

Alzheimer's is the most prevalent form of dementia, a generic term for memory loss and other cognitive skills bad enough to interfere with everyday living. Alzheimer's disease accounts for 60-80 percent of dementia cases.
The greatest known risk factor is increasing age, and the majority of people with Alzheimer's are 65 and older. Alzheimer's disease is regarded to be younger-onset Alzheimer's if it strikes a person under 65. Younger-onset may also be referred to as early-onset Alzheimer's. People with younger-onset Alzheimer's might be in the early, medium, or late stage of the illness.

Alzheimer's progresses with time. Alzheimer's is a progressive illness when dementia symptoms steadily deteriorate over years. In its early stages, memory loss is minimal, but with late-stage Alzheimer's, people lose the capacity to carry on a conversation and react to their surroundings. On average, a person with Alzheimer's lives 4 to 8 years following diagnosis but may live as long as 20 years, depending on other circumstances.

What Causes Alzheimer's Disease?

People who have Alzheimer's disease are frequently older, but the condition isn't a natural part of aging. Scientists aren't sure why some individuals get it and others don't. But scientists do know that the symptoms it produces appear to arise from two basic forms of nerve damage:

Nerve cells develop tangles, termed neurofibrillary tangles.
Protein deposits called beta-amyloid plaques grow up in the brain.

Alzheimer's-Brain-Cells
Experts aren't clear on what causes this damage or how it occurs, but it might be a protein in the blood called ApoE (for apolipoprotein E), which the body utilizes to transport cholesterol in the blood.

There are a few kinds of ApoE that may be associated with an increased risk of Alzheimer's. It might be that some kinds of it induce brain damage. Some experts suspect it has a role in developing the plaques in the brains of patients with Alzheimer's.

Whether or if ApoE partially causes Alzheimer's, genes virtually likely have a role in the illness. Someone with a parent who has the condition is more likely to get it, too.

There is some evidence that those with high blood pressure and high cholesterol have an increased likelihood of having Alzheimer's. More infrequently, brain traumas may be a factor, too — the more serious they are, the higher the risk of Alzheimer's later in life.

Scientists are currently exploring many of these possibilities, but it's known that the major hazards associated with Alzheimer's disease are growing older and having Alzheimer's in your family.

Nearly everyone with Alzheimer's disease will ultimately experience the same symptoms — memory loss, disorientation, problems performing once-familiar activities, and making judgments. While the way of the disease development remains unknown, all varieties of Alzheimer's seem to share overproduction and/or impaired clearance of a kind of protein termed amyloid beta peptides.

Alzheimer's as a Continuum

Alzheimer's disease advances in phases, with the severity of symptoms increasing over time. Alzheimer's has no cure, but one medication — aducanumab (Aduhelm™) — is the first therapy to indicate that eliminating amyloid, one of the hallmarks of Alzheimer's disease, from the brain is fairly likely to prevent cognitive and functional deterioration in persons living with early Alzheimer's.

Other therapies may temporarily delay the severity of dementia symptoms and enhance the quality of life for persons with Alzheimer's and their caretakers. Today, there is a global effort going to identify new methods to treat the condition, postpone its start and prevent it from forming.

Symptoms of Alzheimer's

The most prevalent early indication of Alzheimer's is trouble remembering recently acquired information.

Just like the rest of our bodies, our brains change as we age. Most of us ultimately notice some slowed thinking and occasional issues with remembering particular things. However, substantial memory loss, disorientation, and other dramatic changes in the way our thoughts operate may be an indication that brain cells are deteriorating.

Alzheimer's alterations often begin in the area of the brain that controls learning. As Alzheimer's progresses through the brain it leads to progressively symptoms, such as disorientation, mood, and behavior changes; intensifying confusion about events, time, and place; baseless suspicions about family, friends, and caregivers; more severe memory loss and behavior changes; and speech problems, ingesting and walking.

People with memory loss or other probable indicators of Alzheimer's may find it hard to identify they have a problem. Signs of dementia may be more visible to family members or friends. Anyone having dementia-like signs should consult a doctor as soon as possible.

Earlier diagnostic and intervention approaches are increasing considerably, and treatment choices and sources of support may enhance the quality of life.

Alzheimer's is not the sole cause of memory loss Many individuals have difficulties with memory – this does NOT guarantee they have Alzheimer's. There are numerous distinct reasons for memory loss. If you or someone you know is having signs of dementia, it is advisable to consult a doctor so the reason can be established.

Alzheimer's and the brain

Microscopic changes in the brain occur long before the first indications of memory loss.

The brain contains 100 billion nerve cells (neurons) (neurons). Each nerve cell communicates with several others to build communication networks. Groups of nerve cells have distinct responsibilities. Some are important in thinking, learning, and remembering. Others assist us to see, hear and smell.

To conduct their task, brain cells behave like miniature factories. They acquire supplies, create energy, build equipment and get rid of garbage. Cells also process and store information and interact with other cells. Keeping everything operating takes coordination as well as vast quantities of fuel and oxygen.

Scientists think Alzheimer's illness hinders components of a cell's manufacturing from working efficiently. They are not clear where the crisis begins. But much like a real factory, backups and malfunctions in one system produce issues in other areas. As damage spreads, cells lose their capacity to execute their duties and, ultimately die, creating permanent alterations in the brain.

The function of plaques and tangles

Two aberrant formations termed plaques and tangles are primary suspects in harming and killing nerve cells.

Plaques are collections of a protein fragment termed beta-amyloid (BAY-tuh AM-uh-loyd) that grow up in the gaps between nerve cells.
Tangles are twisted threads of another protein called tau (rhymes with "wow") that pile up within cells.
Three photos of brains, one with a few tangles, another with moderate tangles, and the third with substantial tangles.

Though postmortem studies suggest that most individuals produce some plaques and tangles as they age, those with Alzheimer's tend to develop significantly more and in a predictable manner, starting in the areas critical for memory before spreading to other regions.

Scientists do not know precisely what function plaques and tangles play in Alzheimer's disease.

Most specialists think they somehow play a vital role in inhibiting communication among nerve cells and altering processes that cells need to live.

It's the deterioration and death of nerve cells that causes memory impairment, personality changes, trouble carrying out everyday tasks, and other signs of Alzheimer's disease.

Research and progress

In 1906, German physician Dr. Alois Alzheimer initially diagnosed "a unique illness" - one of significant memory loss and tiny brain abnormalities — a sickness we now know as Alzheimer's.

Today, Alzheimer's is at the heart of biomedical research. Researchers are striving to reveal as many facets of Alzheimer's disease and other dementias as feasible. Some of the most astounding advances have provided information on how Alzheimer's affects the brain. The goal is this increased knowledge will lead to novel therapies. Many possible techniques are now being researched internationally

Chapter 2: Stages of Alzheimer's illness

Alzheimer's disease tends to begin slowly and steadily worsens over many years. Eventually, Alzheimer's disease affects most sections of your brain. Memory, reasoning, judgment, language, problem-solving, personality, and mobility may all be impaired by the condition.

There are five phases connected with Alzheimer's disease:preclinical Alzheimer's disease, mild cognitive impairment due to Alzheimer's disease, mild dementia due to Alzheimer's disease, moderate dementia due to Alzheimer's disease, and severe dementia due to Alzheimer's disease.

Dementia is a word used to describe a set of symptoms that degrade intellectual and social skills sufficient enough to impede everyday life.

The five Alzheimer's phases might help you comprehend what can happen, but it's crucial to note that these stages are simply approximate generalizations. The sickness is an ongoing process. Each individual has a varied experience with Alzheimer's and its symptoms.

Preclinical Alzheimer's disease

Alzheimer's disease develops long before any symptoms become visible. This stage is termed preclinical Alzheimer's disease, and it's normally found exclusively in research settings. You won't notice symptoms at this time, nor will people around you.

This stage of Alzheimer's may endure for years or even decades. Although you won't notice any changes, modern imaging technology may now show deposits of a protein called amyloid-beta which is a characteristic of Alzheimer's disease. The capacity to detect these early deposits may be very significant for clinical trials and in the future when novel therapies are developed for Alzheimer's disease.

Additional biomarkers — indicators that potentially indicate an elevated risk of illness — have been found for Alzheimer's disease. These biomarkers may be used to support the diagnosis of Alzheimer's disease, generally, after symptoms occur.

Genetic testing also may tell you whether you have a greater chance of Alzheimer's disease, especially early-onset Alzheimer's disease. These tests aren't advised for everyone, but you and your doctor may consider if genetic testing would be useful for you.

When with better imaging methods, biomarkers and genetic testing will become increasingly significant as novel therapies for Alzheimer's disease are produced.

Mild cognitive impairment (MCI) owing to Alzheimer's disease

People with moderate cognitive impairment have minimal abnormalities in their memory and reasoning capacity. These changes aren't substantial enough to disrupt jobs or relationships yet. People with MCI may suffer memory gaps when it comes to information that is typically readily recalled, such as discussions, recent occurrences, or appointments.

People with MCI may also have difficulties assessing the amount of time required for a task, or they may have difficulty properly judging the number or sequence of steps needed to finish a job. The capacity to make informed judgments might become difficult for those with MCI.

Not everyone with modest cognitive impairment has Alzheimer's disease. MCI is generally diagnosed based on the doctor's examination of symptoms and professional opinion. But if required, the same tests used to detect preclinical Alzheimer's disease may assist in deciding if MCI is related to Alzheimer's disease or something else.

Mild dementia linked to Alzheimer's disease

Alzheimer's disease is frequently diagnosed in the mild dementia stage, when it becomes evident to family and professionals that a person is experiencing substantial difficulties with memory and thinking that disrupts everyday functioning.

In the mild dementia stage, persons may experience:

Memory loss of recent occurrences. Individuals may have a particularly hard time recalling recently taught knowledge and ask the same question again and over.

Difficulty with problem-solving, complicated activities, and sound decisions. Planning a family gathering or handling a budget may seem daunting. Many individuals encounter failures in judgment, such as when making financial judgments.

Personality changes. People may become quiet or distant — particularly in socially demanding settings — or display unexpected impatience or hostility. Reduced drive to accomplish activities also is typical.

Difficulty organizing and conveying ideas. Finding the correct words to explain items or accurately communicate concepts becomes tougher.

Getting missing or misplacing items. Individuals have greater problems finding their way around, especially in familiar settings. It's also typical to lose or misplace stuff, particularly costly goods.

Moderate dementia related to Alzheimer's disease

During the moderate dementia stage of Alzheimer's disease, individuals get increasingly confused and forgetful and begin to require more support with everyday tasks and self-care.

People with the mild dementia stage of Alzheimer's disease may:

Show progressively poor judgment and developing bewilderment. Individuals lose track of where they are, the day of the week, or the season. They may confuse family members or close friends with one another or mistake strangers for relatives.

They may roam, presumably in pursuit of situations that seem more familiar. These challenges make it risky to leave persons in the mild dementia stage on their own.

Experience even more memory loss. People may forget pieces of their personal history, such as their home or phone number, or where they attended school. They repeat favorite tales or make new ones to cover holes in memory.

Need assistance with certain regular duties. Assistance may be necessary with selecting adequate attire for the occasion or the weather and with showering, grooming, using the restroom, and other self-care. Some people sometimes lose control of their bladder or bowel motions.

Undergo major changes in personality and conduct. It's fairly rare during the intermediate dementia stage for individuals to acquire baseless suspicions — for example, to become persuaded that friends, relatives, or professional caretakers are taking from them or that a spouse is having an affair. Others may see or hear things that aren't really there.

Individuals sometimes get restless or disturbed, particularly late in the day. Some individuals may experience bouts of hostile physical conduct.

Severe dementia related to Alzheimer's disease

In the late stage of the illness, dubbed severe dementia due to Alzheimer's disease, mental performance continues to diminish, and the disease has a significant influence on mobility and physical capacities.

In late stage severe dementia owing to Alzheimer's disease, persons generally:

Lose the capacity to speak clearly. A person can no longer talk or speak in ways that make sense, but he or she may sometimes utter words or phrases.

Require daily help with personal care. This includes entire support with eating, dressing, using the restroom, and all other everyday self-care duties.

Experience a deterioration in physical capacities. A person may become unable to walk without help, then unable to sit or hold up his or her head without support. Muscles may become stiff and reflex aberrant.
Eventually, a person loses the capacity to swallow and regulate bladder and stool movements.

Rate of progression through Alzheimer's disease stages

The pace of advancement for Alzheimer's disease varies greatly. On average, persons with Alzheimer's disease live between three and 11 years following diagnosis, although some survive 20 years or more. The degree of disability upon diagnosis may decrease life expectancy. Untreated vascular risk factors such as hypertension are connected with a higher rate of advancement of Alzheimer's disease.

Pneumonia is a major cause of mortality because poor swallowing causes food or drinks to enter the lungs, where an infection may develop. Various prevalent reasons for mortality include dehydration, malnutrition, falls, and other infections.

Chapter 3: CAREGIVING

Stages and Behaviors

As Alzheimer's and other dementias deteriorate, routines change—as does your role as caregiver. While adjustments in behavior could be onerous, we give resources to help you through each stage of the illness.

Accepting the Diagnosis
Accepting a diagnosis of Alzheimer's or a related condition demands time to assimilate information.

Early-Stage Caregiving
Early-stage Alzheimer's and related dementia symptoms are modest and the main function of a caregiver is support.

Middle-Stage Caregiving

During the final stages of Alzheimer's, the individual living with dementia will demand a significant quantity of care.

Late-Stage Caregiving

The late stage of Alzheimer's typically demands special care. As a caregiver, your obligation is to safeguard the quality of life and dignity.

Aggression and Anger

Aggressive acts could arise fast, with no obvious explanation, or evolve from an unpleasant event.

Anxiety and Agitation

A person with dementia may feel restless or upset in certain environments when focused on specific characteristics.

Depression

Identifying depression in someone with Alzheimer's may be tricky, since dementia may generate some of the same symptoms.

Hallucinations

Some hallucinations may seem alarming to a person with Alzheimer's, while others may feature common scenes from the past.

Memory Loss and Confusion

Those with Alzheimer's may not remember familiar individuals, places, or items in the final stages of the condition.

Repetition

In most instances, a person with Alzheimer's is probably striving for comfort, stability, and familiarity when repeating information.

Sleep Issues and Sundowning

Like changes in memory and behavior, sleep issues somehow emerge from the effect of Alzheimer's on the brain.

Suspicions and Delusions

Suspicions and delusions — firmly held ideas about things that are not real — may occur in middle- to late-stage Alzheimer's.

Wandering
Wandering among adults with dementia is hazardous, but there are techniques and services to assist avoid it.

Alzheimer's disease (AD) is a neurodegenerative disorder characterized by cognitive and behavioral impairment that substantially interferes with social and occupational functioning. It is an incurable sickness with a lengthy preclinical stage and progressive development.

In AD, plaques develop in the hippocampus, a region deep in the brain that helps to retain memories, and in other parts of the cerebral cortex that are important in thinking and making decisions. If plaques themselves cause AD or if they are a by-product of the AD process remains unknown.

Who has Alzheimer's Disease?

Percentage of adults aged 65 and older with Alzheimer's disease by race and ethnicity 14 percent African Americans, 12 percent Hispanics, 10 percent non-Hispanic white.
In 2020, as many as 5.8 million Americans were battling Alzheimer's disease.

Younger adults may get Alzheimer's disease, but it is less frequent.
The number of persons living with the illness doubles every 5 years beyond age 65.
This number is predicted to practically treble to 14 million persons by 2060.

Symptoms of the condition might start to appear after age 60, and the risk rises with age.

What is known about Alzheimer's Disease?

Scientists do not yet entirely know what causes Alzheimer's disease. There likely is not a single answer but rather numerous elements that might affect each individual differently.

Age is the greatest established risk factor for Alzheimer's disease.
Family history—researchers assume that genetics may play a role in developing Alzheimer's disease. However, genes do not equal destiny. A healthy lifestyle may help lower your probability of obtaining Alzheimer's disease. Two major, long-term studies demonstrate that adequate physical activity, a decent diet, moderate alcohol consumption, and avoiding smoking may assist people.

Changes in the brain might occur years before the first symptoms show.

Researchers are exploring whether education, nutrition, and environment have a role in developing Alzheimer's disease.

There is rising scientific evidence that healthy activities, which have been demonstrated to protect against cancer, diabetes, and heart disease, may also lessen the risk for subjective cognitive decline.

What are the warning indications of Alzheimer's disease?

Alzheimer's disease is not a natural part of aging. Memory impairments are often one of the early warning signs of Alzheimer's disease and associated dementias.

In addition to cognitive difficulties, someone with signs of Alzheimer's disease may encounter one or more of the following:

- Memory loss that hinders routine functioning, such as becoming lost in a familiar setting or repeating questions.
- Trouble managing money and making bills.
- Difficulty doing routine tasks at home, at work, or at leisure.
- Decreased or poor judgment.
- Misplacing items and being unable to retrace steps to locate them.
- Changes in mood, attitude, or action.

Even if you or someone you know has some or even most of these signs, it doesn't suggest it's Alzheimer's disease.

What to do if you suspect Alzheimer's illness

Getting evaluated by your healthcare practitioner may help identify whether the symptoms you are experiencing are connected to Alzheimer's disease or more manageable diseases such as a vitamin deficiency or a side effect from the drug. Early and accurate diagnosis also gives chances for you and your family to consider financial planning, make advance directives, participate in clinical trials, and anticipate care requirements.

How is Alzheimer's illness treated?

Medical treatment may enhance the quality of life for those living with Alzheimer's disease and for their caretakers. There is presently no recognized cure for Alzheimer's disease.

Treatment targets numerous areas:

- Helping individuals sustain brain health.
- Managing behavioral symptoms.
- Slowing or postponing indications of the ailment.
- Support for family and friends

Currently, many individuals living with Alzheimer's disease are cared for at home by family members. Caregiving may have good aspects for the caregiver as well as the person being cared for. It may offer personal joy to the caregiver, such as satisfaction from assisting a family member or friend, and lead to the development of new talents and enhanced familial bonds.

Although most folks happily give care to their loved ones and friends, caring for a person with Alzheimer's disease at home may be a demanding effort and may get overwhelming at times. Each day offers new difficulties as the caregiver copes with varying degrees of competence and new patterns of behavior. As the condition becomes worse, persons living with Alzheimer's disease often require more extensive care.

What is the burden of Alzheimer's disease in the United States?

Alzheimer's disease is one of the top 10 main causes of death in the United States.

The 6th greatest cause of mortality among US adults.
The 5th major cause of mortality among persons aged 65 years or older.
In 2020, an estimated 5.8 million Americans aged 65 years or older had Alzheimer's disease.
This figure is anticipated to almost quadruple to 14 million individuals by 2060.

In 2010, the costs for treating Alzheimer's disease were estimated to range between $159 and $215 billion. By 2040, these expenditures are estimated to grow to between $379 and more than $500 billion annually.

Death rates for Alzheimer's disease are growing, unlike heart disease and cancer death rates that are on the upswing. Dementia, including Alzheimer's disease, is under-reported on death certificates and hence the proportion of older individuals who die from Alzheimer's may be significantly higher.

What is known about minimizing your risk of Alzheimer's Disease?

The research on risk reduction is fast advancing, and considerable breakthroughs are within grasp. For example, there is mounting evidence that adults who follow great lifestyle behaviors — including regular exercise and blood pressure control — may minimize their risk of dementia.

There is rising scientific evidence that healthy activities, which have been demonstrated to protect against cancer, diabetes, and heart disease, may also lessen the risk for subjective cognitive decline.

What Happens to the Brain in Alzheimer's Disease?

The healthy human brain comprises tens of billions of neurons—specialized cells that process and transfer information through electrical and chemical impulses. They convey information between various areas of the brain, and from the brain to the muscles and organs of the body. Alzheimer's disease impairs this communication among neurons, resulting in loss of function and cell death.

Chapter 4: Food and Eating

Regular, healthy meals may become a struggle for persons living in the medium and late stages of Alzheimer's. They may feel overwhelmed with too many food options, forget to eat, or assume they have already eaten.

- Nutrition tips
- Make mealtimes quiet and pleasant
- Encourage independence
- Minimize eating and nutrition issues

Nutrition tips
Black family dining together, with a lady placing salad on a plate that a guy is carrying for an elderly woman, Proper nutrition is necessary to maintain the body robust and healthy.

For a person with Alzheimer's or dementia, an inadequate diet may aggravate behavioral symptoms and promote weight loss.

The simple dietary advice below may assist increase the person with dementia's health and your health as a caregiver, too.

Provide a balanced diet with a range of foods. Offer veggies, fruits, whole grains, low-fat dairy items, and lean protein meals.

Limit foods with high saturated fat and cholesterol. Some fat is important for health – but not all fats are equal. Go low on fats that are detrimental to heart health, such as butter, solid shortening, lard, and fatty cuts of meat.

Cut down on refined sugars. Often found in processed meals, refined sugars provide calories but lack vitamins, minerals, and fiber. You may control a sweet desire with healthy choices like fruit or juice-sweetened baked products.

But note that in the later stages of Alzheimer's, if appetite loss is a concern, adding sugar to meals may increase eating.

Limit meals with high sodium and use less salt. Most individuals in the United States eat too much salt, which impacts blood pressure.
As an alternative, add spices or herbs to season meals.
People with Alzheimer's or dementia do not require a particular diet.
As with anybody, eating a well-balanced, healthy diet is vital for general health.

As the condition advances, loss of appetite and weight loss may become issues. In such circumstances, the doctor may advise supplements between meals to provide calories.

Staying hydrated may also be a difficulty. Encourage fluid intake by giving small cups of water or other liquids throughout the day or meals with high water content, such as fruit, soups, milkshakes, and smoothies.

Possible reasons for poor appetite

Not recognizing food. The individual may no longer recognize the meals you place on his or her plate.

Poor-fitting dentures. Eating may be painful, but the individual may not be able to tell you this. Make sure dentures fit and see the dentist periodically.

Medications. New drugs or a dose modification may influence appetite. If you see a difference, contact the doctor.

Not enough exercise. Lack of physical exercise will diminish appetite. Encourage easy activities, such as going for a stroll, gardening, or cleaning dishes.

Decreased perception of smell and taste. The person with dementia may not eat since food may not smell or taste as wonderful as it previously did.

Make mealtimes quiet and pleasant

During the middle stages of Alzheimer's, distractions, too many options, and changes in perception, taste and smell may make eating more challenging. The following tips may help:

Limit distractions. Serve meals in peaceful circumstances, away from the television and other distractions.

Keep the table arrangement basic. Avoid patterned dishes, tablecloths and placemats that can mislead the individual. Using color to contrast plates against a tablecloth or placemat might make it simpler for the user to discern the food from the plate or table.

Consider using a plastic tablecloth, napkins or aprons to make cleaning simpler. Provide just the utensils required for the meal to minimize misunderstanding.

Distinguish food from the plate. Changes in visual and spatial ability may make it challenging for someone with dementia to separate food from the plate or the dish from the table. It might help to use white plates or bowls with a contrasting color placemat. Avoid patterned plates, tablecloths, and placemats.

Check the food temperature. A person living with dementia may not be able to detect whether something is excessively hot to eat or drink.

Always test the temperature of meals and drinks before serving them.

Offer one food item at a time. The individual may be unable to choose among the meals on his or her plate. Serve just one or two things at a time. For example, serve mashed potatoes followed by the main meal.

Be flexible with culinary choices. It is conceivable the individual may suddenly acquire particular eating preferences or reject meals he or she may have loved in the past.

Allow plenty of time to eat. Keep in mind that it might take an hour or more for the individual to complete.

Eat together. Give the individual the chance to dine with others. Keeping mealtimes sociable might encourage the individual to eat.

Keep in mind the individual may not recall when or whether he or she ate. If the individual continues to inquire about having breakfast, try providing many breakfasts – juice, followed by toast, followed by cereal.
Map out a strategy to address Alzheimer's

Encourage independence

During the middle stage of Alzheimer's, let the person with dementia remain as autonomous as feasible during meals. Be ready to aid, when required.

Make the most of the person's ability. Adapting serving plates and equipment to make dining simpler. You may serve food in a bowl instead of on a plate, or try using a plate with rims or protecting edges. A spoon with a big handle may be less difficult to manage than a fork or even allow the individual to use his or her hands if it's easier.

Serve finger appetizers. Try bite-sized items that are simple to pick up, such as chicken nuggets, salmon sticks, tuna sandwiches, orange segments, steamed broccoli, or cauliflower pieces. Or create a meal in the shape of a sandwich to make it simpler for the individual to feed herself or herself.

Try hand-over-hand feeding. Demonstrate eating behavior by putting a utensil in the person's hand, placing your hand around theirs, and elevating both of your hands to the person's mouth for a mouthful.

Don't bother about neatness. Let the individual feed himself or herself as much as possible. Set bowls and plates on a non-skid surface such as a cloth or towel. Use cups and mugs with lids to avoid spillage. Fill glasses half full and use flexible straws.

Minimize eating and nutrition issues
In the middle and late stages of Alzheimer's, swallowing issues may lead to choking and weight loss. Be mindful of safety hazards and attempt these tips:

Prepare meals so they aren't hard to chew or swallow. Grind meals, chop them into bite-size pieces, or offer soft foods (applesauce, cottage cheese, and scrambled eggs) (applesauce, cottage cheese, and scrambled eggs).

Be watchful for indications of choking. Avoid meals that are difficult to chew fully, such as raw carrots. Encourage the individual to sit up straight with his or her head slightly forward. If the person's head tilts backward, move it to a forward posture. After the meal, inspect the person's mouth to make sure food has been swallowed. Learn the Heimlich technique in case of an emergency.

Address a reduced appetite. If the individual has a lower appetite, try making some of his or her favorite dishes. You may also explore boosting the person's physical activity or preparing numerous little meals rather than three big meals